Walking Out of the
I Was into the I AM

Brenda T. Vaughn

Heart of God International Outreach Ministries

PO. Box 162095

Atlanta Ga. 30321

heartofgodoutreachministries@gmail.com

Copyright

Walking out of the I Was into the I Am © 2020

Brenda T. Vaughn

Printed in the United States of America

Acknowledgement

I want to Thank You, Lord, for all you have done. I thank you for the blessings you have manifested in my life. I would like to thank all of my family, friends, and loved ones for being there for me. Thank you for all of your support, love, patience, and dedication as we all grow in the ministry.

Table of Content

Introduction

As you read this book, you will begin to understand the difference between the "I Was" and the "I AM." You will learn that you have the victory through Christ Jesus, and your life will never be the same. Once you've received Christ, your journey and your new walk begins. Your old life has been wiped away; you have a new life. God has cleansed and wiped away yours sins. Now, you are able to walk and have a balanced life, and your steps are ordered by the Lord.

For many years, I have been in the ministry. Over that time, I have seen and experienced the move of God threw healing, deliverance, and miracles by the power of the Holy Spirit. I have seen lives transformed from the "I Was" into the "I AM."

In my personal life, I have encountered a very powerful move of God, where I was also transformed from the "I Was" into the "I Am." I had to be renewed in my mind. There were times when the enemy was trying to take my mind and take me down that road of darkness. This is where I had to totally depend on God to help me walk away from the "I Was." I had to totally trust God and stand completely on His word. I had to make a sound decision to follow Christ. Now that I am walking in the "I Am," I have to believe that God can transform my life and my mind.

"Having faith and a good conscience, some have rejected these and have shipwrecked their faith." 1 Timothy 1: 19 (CSB)

CHAPTER 1
THE I WAS:
MY YOUTH

As a child, I grew up living under the roof of two pastors. I was raised by my great auntie and uncle. They filled my cup with what they had. They had very little to pour out. I thought their teaching was always right. Although, I didn't always abide by their rules.

During those years, we were in church twenty-four seven. We had programs for everything: women's day, men's day,

Pastor's appreciation day; the different choirs had their own programs, the deacon board, the mother board, the hospitality team, bake sales, and fish fries. The list goes on and on. When I looked back, I had to ask myself, "Where was the Holy Spirit in all of that?"

You see, I didn't learn all I know now when I was young. Later, I learned I had very little knowledge of the Holy Spirit. I also realized there were some family members that knew. Maybe they didn't know it all, but they knew more than I was taught. In addition, the explanations were conflicting between the ministers in the family. There were so many of them. Some believed in the Holy Spirit, and some just believed in God and Jesus being the Son of God. They believed Jesus went to the cross and that was it.

Every Easter (now called Resurrection Sunday), I hoped for a big Easter egg hunt on Saturday and looked forward to saying my Easter speech on Sunday. That was about it. I would recite, "I came here today to wish you a Happy Easter Day." I just knew that was the good life.

Also, during those years, I experienced some traumatic things. Some of them my family knew about and others they didn't. As a child, I was molested. I never told anyone; I held it for years. Then, as a teenager, I was raped, and my family did know about that either. I had to go to the hospital and the police station. During that incident, I had to fight for my life. I was beaten and choked. When my family learned about it, they blamed me. They didn't understand because neither one of them had been through such a thing. Those kinds of things just didn't happen back then.

When I attempted to explain it to them, they didn't seem to care. Then, I met a lady. She was understanding and compassionate. I could talk to her when I couldn't talk to anybody else. She was very special to me because she helped me through my pain.

As time passed, I began to feel angry because my mother passed when I was only four. I wanted to understand why she was not there to protect me. My father was there physically, but that was it.

My family believed I had done something to cause those bad things to happen to me. Even some of the men at church would try to hit on me from time to time. I would hold it all in, but my anger got worse and worse.

As I grew older, I began to recognize a lot in our family church and other churches, as God led me years later, from the smallest to the largest. I had to learn to forgive my family, but I had yet to learn how to walk in true relationship with God.

Even though I attended church, I still lived my life the way I wanted. I thought I had it going on. After being on welfare for some time, I soon landed a good job. I was excited to be living what I thought was "the life." I would dress up and go to work smelling good, and I felt I was looking good. I was making good money, and I wasn't on welfare anymore.

Every night, I would get prepared for bed. Then, I would enjoy a shot of Brandy and a cigarette at my bed side to relax me from the stress of the day.

The next morning, I would make a pot of coffee, put a cap of Brandy in it and go to work at the hotel where I was a manager. My job was to make sure all the rooms were cleaned. Yes, I was still attending church every Sunday because that's what many people did.

I had yet to be introduced to the Holy Spirit. I was walking in the "I Was" and was comfortable there for a while. Then, one day, God began to nudge me.

<u>Scripture Reference:</u>

1 Corinthians 6:19 states, "Don't you realize that your body is the temple of the Holy Spirit, who lives in you and was given to you by God? You do not belong to yourself" (NLT).

"May the Lord direct your hearts to God's love and Christ's endurance," 2 Thessalonians 3: 5 (CSB).

CHAPTER 2
WHAT IS THE "I WAS?"

When I talk about stepping out of the "I Was," I'm referring to walking away from your past. I will use myself as an example.

As stated previously, I was that person who enjoyed living a life of entertainment. I loved having people around me drinking brandy, smoking cigarettes, and more. I would cook and invite people over just to have a good time.

Those are some examples of walking in the "I Was." When you're there, you may find it difficult to stop. In addition, you may find it hard to come out of certain relationships because you want to hold on to the past. I continued to go back to the same kind of relationships, even those with the men who were not good for me, but I had grown used to them. It didn't matter how bad they treated me: disrespectful, cheating, hitting, and lying.

These are a few of the areas where we get stuck, and we don't want to move forward. It took me years to realize that I was repeating a cycle over and over again. At one point, I thought that was the way I was supposed to live. I was living a life I didn't understand. I had been married twice and the cycle of disrespect continued. It wasn't until I got tired of the same old thing. Every woman has that dream of the house with the fence around it, yet you can be living a dream but sleep walking at the same time, not knowing who you are. I was moving around doing my everyday activities at home, on my job, in church, and around my friends. I questioned myself, yet I remained there until I realized something was wrong, and it was time to change.

We can camouflage our life to make it look like the real thing. We can have people thinking our grass is green when it's not grass at all; it's artificial turf. I had a fake life. It looked good but it wasn't. I lived a fantasy life. That type of life makes us believe we are good when we are not. Sometimes, we live that life for so long that we feel comfortable staying there until things get crazy. That is what happened to me. There is a difference in living in the "I Was" versus walking in the "I Am." I talked about my life and how I thought I was living life to the fullest. You see, you can have it all and be miserable.

One day, I was at home watching a gospel T.V. station, not sure who of the name of the individual, but I remember the minister speaking a word from the LORD. He shared, "God is instructing you to let it go. You need to make a sound decision and make it today." That was during the time God was calling me to totally give my life over to Him. I had not slept in two weeks. I was really fighting. I wanted to sleep but I couldn't. He was calling me, but I wanted to stay in the life I was used to living. I thought I would have a boring life, and I didn't want that. I had to give my life over to God if I wanted to sleep. Walking out of the "I Was" may take some time, even years, because there are things in our lives that may try to grip us. The great thing about it is that we can walk away from pieces of the "I Was" each day. We must remember that each day is a new beginning, a choice to walk away from yesterday's failures and disappointments. Once we understand that Christ died just for us, we will recognize that the old life has to go, even if we messed up yesterday, leave it in the past and walk in the "I Am."

Scripture Reference:

"Therefore, if anyone is in Christ, the new creation has come: The old has gone, the new is here. 2 Corinthians 5: 17 (NIV)

"I am the Lord your God, who brought you out of Egypt, out of the land of slavery." Exodus 20:2 (NIV)

"So do not fear, for I am with you; do not be dismayed, for I am your God. I will strengthen you and help you; I will uphold you with my righteous right hand." Isaiah 41:10 (NIV)

"When Jesus spoke again to the people, he said, 'I am the light of the world. Whoever follows me will never walk in darkness but will have the light of life.'" John 8:12 (NIV)

"I am the bread of life." John 6:48 (NIV)

You must believe that you will change, and you will. Believe and have faith.

Have you let go of the "I Was?"

_____

_____

_____

_____

_____

_____

_____

_____

_____

_____

_____

_____

_____

_____

_____

_____

_____

_____

_____

_____

CHAPTER 3
WHAT HINDERS US IN THE "I WAS"

There are several things that may hinder our decision to change and move forward in God: negativity, control, toxic relationships, and negative thinking.

Letting go of negative relationships can be tough. They can even become strongholds. Let's begin by looking at the word. Since God created Adam and Eve, He has desired us to be in healthy relationships: mind, body and spirit. God created us to have positive relationships with one another. However, sometimes, we invite the wrong people into our lives, and those people are not positive. They don't bring anything healthy; only negative conversation, doubt, frustration, anger and disappointment.

We've all had individuals who have tried to cause us harm, trying to play with our mind, emotions, and bringing negative energy. Those individuals drain you mentally, physically and spiritually. Those types of relationships bring about stress. When you are in the mist of negative relationships, you must totally depend on God and His favor. Only God can move people out of your life, and they will never return again.

"Moses answered the people, "Do not be afraid. Stand firm and you will see the deliverance the Lord will bring you today. The Egyptians you see today you will never see again." Exodus 14:13 (NIV)

What negative relationships are you still in and are afraid of letting go?

_____

_____

_____

_____

_____

_____

_____

_____

_____

_____

_____

_____

_____

_____

_____

_____

_____

_____

_____

_____

_____

Letting go of Controlling Relationships

A controlling relationship comes in several different varieties of gift-wrapped paper. The spirit of control even runs deep, in and outside of the ministry, where they want to control your relationships. Even when it comes down to your family, they try to tell you where you can and can't go. This kind of control can be frustrating.

A controlling spirit may hinder you from letting go because of the bondage you're in. It keeps you from allowing God to meet your needs and keeps you from moving forward in the "I Am."

Sometimes, we even close our eyes to the signs that are right before us. Then, we find ourselves deeper and deeper in it. We have one eye open and one closed. We may have lowered our standards and accepted the behavior.

Scripture Reference:

"Being confident of this, that he who began a good work in you will carry it on to completion until the day of Christ Jesus." Philippians 1:6 (NIV)

What person's or things are controlling or hindering you from walking away from a relationship?

_____

_____

_____

_____

_____

_____

_____

_____

_____

_____

_____

_____

_____

_____

_____

_____

_____

_____

_____

_____

_____

_____

_____

_____

_____

_____

_____

_____

_____

_____

_____

_____

_____

_____

_____

_____

_____

_____

_____

_____

_____

_____

_____

_____

Letting go of a Toxic Relationship

We all have been in a toxic relationship, and sometimes they can be very damaging. Being in a toxic relationship, you may feel that you are not good enough and never will be.

In addition, when you are in this type of relationship, there are always criticisms no matter what you do. It's not about you and your good qualities; it's all about trying to break you down. When they try to break you down, they are trying to gain the upper hand. They intend to make you feel insecure.

This kind of toxic behavior is not Christ like. In this type of situation, staying in the "I Was" can hold you back for years. You must gain the strength to walk away and into the "I Am." You have to have a sound mind to make a sound decision.

Scripture Reference:

"I can do all things through him who gives me

Strength." Philippians 4:13 (NIV)

"The heart of man plans his way, but the

Lord establishes his steps. Proverbs 16:9 (ESV)

What are some of the toxic relationships or things that you are afraid to make a sound decision about?

_____

_____

_____

_____

_____

_____

_____

_____

_____

_____

_____

_____

_____

_____

_____

_____

_____

_____

Letting go of Negative Thinking

Negative thinking is where I was at one point in my life. I get it, if all you've had in your life is disappointment, if you don't get anything else from this book, I pray you realize that negative thinking can dominate your mind, causing you to never move forward. Wherever your mind is, that is the way your life will be. The enemy will keep bringing things, situations, circumstances, and the type of people who have the same kind of mine set. You have to use the word of God against that negative spirit. It also keeps you from being blessed. Yes, you are blessed currently, but you can be blessed even the more. To get rid of my negative spirit, I had to meditate on God's word. At night, I would allow the word to play in my ears. During the day, I would use the word of God, casting down every high imagination that exalted itself against the knowledge of God in my life.

"Casting down imaginations, and every high thing that exalted itself against the knowledge of God and bringing into captivity every thought to the obedience of Christ." 2 Corinthians 10:5 (KJV)

I had to plead and decree the blood of Jesus over my mind, my thoughts, and my body. I had to use the word against the enemy. You must understand, the enemy wants us to stay in that negative mind set because he knows as long as we are walking in the "I Was" we won't get everything that God has for us. As of this day, choose to no longer walk in the "I Was," thinking negative, walk in the "I Am," with Christ. What good could come out of it all? You. You are fearful and wonderfully made.

Just like the question in scripture, "What good can come out of Nineveh?" Here is the answer. It doesn't matter what town or city you reside in, God can and will change the way you think as you get into His word.

To help you along your journey, get around some positive people who will encourage you. It's not going to disappear right away, but you will be well on your way to better ways of thinking.

"Do not conform to the pattern of this world but be transformed by the renewing of your mind. Then you will be able to test and approve what God's will is—his good, pleasing and perfect will." Romans 12:2 (NIV)

What are some of the negative thoughts that hinder you from walking in the "I Am?"

_____

_____

_____

_____

_____

_____

_____

_____

_____

_____

_____

_____

_____

_____

_____

_____

_____

CHAPTER 4
HOW TO OVERCOME THE "I WAS"

Once we come to Christ, we are new creations. Our old lives are gone, and new lives begin. There are several things in our lives that we must do before this takes place. We must totally surrender our lives over to God. Are you willing to surrender? When you make a sound decision to make God your Lord and Savior, your life begins to change. God will began guiding you in the way you should go. You will begin to understand His voice and start to feel uncomfortable about certain places you once felt good about going. You will feel different about a lot of things in your spirit, like what feels right or what feels wrong. The Holy Spirit will lead and guide you every step of the way.

This is the beginning of overcoming the "I Was" in your life. You will begin to walk by faith and trust God that your old life has gone, and your new life has begun. There will be times when family, friends, love ones and the devil will bring up your past, but I want you to know and understand that you are free from your past, and no weapon formed against you shall prosper.

"No weapon forged against you will prevail, and you will refute every tongue that accuses you. This is the heritage of the servants of the Lord, and this is their vindication from me," declares the Lord."
Isaiah 54:17 (NIV)

Once you come to Christ Jesus, all of your sins are in the past. Your present and the future are covered by the blood of Jesus.

This is where a lot of people have fallen back into sin, and they feel that God is mad with them, or they feel God won't help them or that the sin is too big. They feel that God can't or won't forgive them. I am here to tell you that your sin is already forgiven.

Don't hesitate to repent and ask God for forgiveness. In the Bible, there was a woman who had a sinful past. She was caught in adultery. The Pharisees brought the woman to Jesus, and they told Jesus about the woman's sin.

Jesus said, "If any of you who is without sin, let him cast the first stone." We all have sinned and falling short of the glory of God. He is always there. When we sin, all we have to do is ask God for forgiveness, and don't do that thing again. You can always come to him. I had to learn, when walking with Christ, He is not that kind of God who punishes you for everything, neither does He beat you down when you make a mistake.

God will encourage you to do things differently. He is not this mean God who wants to treat us bad. If that were the case, He would have killed us a long time ago. There were times in my life where I messed up, and He spared me over and over again. There were other times when I said things I shouldn't have. God made me aware that it wasn't good to speak that way.

At other times, God would instruct me to do things, but I chose to do them differently, yet he was still there with me. There have been times in all of our lives when God told us to go down a certain road. He might have told us not to hang around certain people, but we continued dealing with them, and then he had to show us why He had given us the instructions. He may have given instructions about a direction to take, and we went the opposite way. Then, we realize there was a roadblock, and that roadblock was going to hinder us from reaching our destination in a timely manner, personally and spiritually. God still works with us even when we are on the wrong road. I'm not telling you to be disobedient, but if you get off track, he won't just throw you to the wolves. We don't always get it right. God wants us to be on the road to success. He will show us through His word, threw others, threw messages, or threw conversations. However, he speaks, He is speaking in love, just stop and listen.

I have overcome the "I Was" of the past.

_____

_____

_____

_____

_____

_____

_____

_____

_____

_____

_____

_____

_____

_____

_____

_____

_____

_____

_____

CHAPTER 5
COMING OUT OF THE I WAS: MY JOURNEY TO FORGIVENESS

Forgiveness was one of the first steps in the process of coming out of the "I Was." I struggled for some time. Eventually, I attended Christian counseling. That was when things started to unfold. I began to understand the power of forgiveness.

When you learn to forgive and let go, you begin to see a change. You can love a person even when you know that person doesn't care for you. When there is unforgiveness, we lose our voice because when we are angry about a situation or a circumstance, it comes out in our voice because we feel bad about ourselves and believe it is our fault. Then, we get angry all over again.

I learned that the spirit of unforgiveness wants to dominate our ability to speak to the problem. It wants to keep us in bondage and wants us to put a bandage over it and not pray so we won't be healed.

In my personal life, I had to look at Jesus and the wounds and bruises he took for me. Then, I said, "Okay, God, I'm turning it all over to you."

Jesus took it all so that I wouldn't have to. As I walked through my experience, I felt I had no voice, but once I forgave, I was able to take my voice back. The enemy wanted me silent. He wanted me to keep patching up the wounds and not being totally delivered from the past.

I didn't forgive for the people that hurt me; I forgave for me. I had to forgive my parents for not being there. I had to forgive my family members. I had to realize that they can only take us so far in life. I learned to look to the cross, the "I Am." Even Jesus on the Cross was praying to God for the ones who had wronged Him, the ones who didn't understand Him, the ones who falsely accused Him, and the ones who took him for granted. When Jesus was on the cross, His body was there but His spirit was with God. His spirit was speaking to

God, The "I Am." His spirit was totally connected to God. This is where we need to be when someone wrongs us or violates our space.

When something happens that I'm not comfortable with, I need to immediately connect that situation or circumstance to the "I Am." That is what Jesus did. This is where the healing begins because we are walking away from the "I Was," (the past).

If it happened a year or a few minutes ago, that's the "I Was." We have now turned it over to the "I AM." Now, we have the victory in our situations or circumstances. The sooner we turn it over to God, the devil won't be able to plant that seed of confusion anymore.

When Jesus was on the cross, it may not have looked like He had the victory, but He did. All power was in His hand. Therefore, when you turn it over to God, you also have the victory.

When I look back over my life, I realize that God knew I was going to go through this, so he sent Jesus to pave the way for me to also forgive. Jesus used His voice. He cried, "Father, forgive them, for they don't know what they are doing." Luke 23:34 (NLT)

When we use our voice, we gain back the power God has put down on the inside.

I now understand that my family didn't know how to handle what I was going through. I had to forgive. I also had to forgive the men that caused me pain and hurt. The enemy meant it for evil, but God has turned it around for His good. At one point in my life, I wore the spirit of shame, but when I decided to forgive, I was able to hold my head up and look a person in their eyes. Before that, I would look down on myself. I worried about what they thought of me. But God!

Scripture Reference:

Romans 5:8 states, "But God showed his great love for us by sending Christ to die for us while we were still sinners" (NLT).

Forgiveness gives us the opportunity to allow God to fight for us threw His son

Jesus Christ. Always remember the shedding of The Blood is what has made us whole.

It's covered under the Blood,

The Blood of Jesus,

The Blood Heals,

The Blood Delivers,

The Blood Sets Us Free.

The Power of Forgiveness Prayer

Father, forgive me for my sins, those known and unknown. I pray that you would heal my wounds and bruises. Don't remove your spirit from me. I want a closer walk with you, "I AM." I thank you for showing me, myself, so I can get it right, so I can make a difference in others' lives, and they will see that light in me.

God, I thank you for giving me my voice back to speak to the issues in my life. Help me not to cover them up because of shame. I ask for a total healing from past hurts and pain. Jesus took the stripes and was wounded for me so that I wouldn't have to. Therefore, I turn it all over to you, even if it comes up again, it is all under the blood of Jesus and by His stripes I'm healed. His Blood covers me.

God, thank you for opening up my eyes so I can see your vision for my life. Amen.

What's on Your Mind?

_____
_____
_____
_____
_____
_____
_____
_____

Who do You Need to Forgive?

_____
_____
_____
_____
_____
_____
_____
_____
_____

CHAPTER 6
MY JOURNEY TO THE "I AM"

As the nudging from God continued, I eventually left my home church. While attending different churches, I saw and heard things I knew weren't right. Therefore, there was no room for the Holy Spirit even if He wanted to come in because I soon learned that the Holy Spirit couldn't dwell in unclean places. I had to learn to allow God to direct me to the right place.

Soon, I joined a church in East Point, Georgia. That is where I finally met the Holy Spirit. It was truly a life changing experience. The Holy Spirit began transforming my life little by little. I began to move from the "I Was" into the "I Am." That was when I received the gift of tongues. I still didn't understand it all and what it was all about. It wasn't until I began sitting under a well-known pastor in Atlanta, Georgia. He taught us about the Holy Spirit. I learned that the Holy Spirit was more than just speaking in tongues. I was taught how to use the gift of tongues, and I totally communicated with the father. God understood what I was saying, even when I didn't know what to pray.

After that experience, I began noticing I wasn't going to the places I used to go, and I wasn't doing the things I used to do, such as when I used to smoke cigarettes and drink brandy.

In addition, I began to recognize the voice of God for myself, and I worked to grow my relationship day after day. It wasn't easy, but it was surely worth it.

CHAPTER 7
KNOWING GOD AS THE "I AM"

The Voice of God
The Voice of Jesus

I would like to introduce you to the character of God and His Son Jesus. As you read and study the word of God from day to day, you will begin to understand His character and be equipped to walk in the "I Am" as you draw closer.

God makes it very clear to His children that He is the "I Am" throughout the Bible.

In Genesis 17:1, God was speaking with Abram. He lets him know that He is the "I Am," God Almighty, The El- Shaddai. This means that no one or anything can ever match Him because He is number 1 (one) and nothing on earth will ever have that kind of power.

In addition, Genesis 26:24 records God appearing to Abram. He says, "I Am the God of your father. Do not be afraid, for I Am with you, and I will bless you and will increase your descendants. They will become a great nation."

In Exodus, Moses was feeling insecure when it came down to speaking. When he was instructed to speak to the Israelites, he was reluctant. Yes, there are times when we feel that we can't measure up to the assignment. The question we ask ourselves, "Who am I? I'm not qualified for that. What would people think?"

We, like Moses, soon realize that we are connected to God, The "I Am." We do qualify.

When we say, "Who am I?" We are telling God we sound like Moses. We need to understand it's not us. We are not the one doing the work. All we have to do is be available.

When the "I Am" is sending you, He has put His seal on it. When I say His seal, I am referring to being sealed with the anointing. We look at what we can't do or what we don't want to do. Moses was only the messenger sent by the "I Am." The one and only had sent Him.

In Exodus 3:14, God continues to give Moses instructions. He says, "When you come unto the children of Israel, tell them the God of your ancestors has sent me." In this verse, God was informing them that He is the I Am, Yahweh. He further tells Moses that He appeared to Abraham, to Isaac, and Jacob as El-Shaddai, God Almighty. He let Moses know that he didn't reveal Himself as the name Yahweh to his forefathers, but He was revealing Himself to them. (I Am is whatever we need God to be).

God's Word is the beginning and the end. God's word has brought so much light and the truth to so many people's lives over the years.

The Voice of God

The voice of God is powerful and is open to all who are willing to receive His Son. God has so many different names. When you look at the "I AM" there are so many different ones. He has proven Himself. Below are just a few of His names that we all can relate to.

1. Jehovah Jireh = The one who sees our needs; He provides for us - Genesis 22:14

2. Jehovah M'kaddesh =The Lord God our sanctification. He sets us apart. I Am the Lord who makes you holy. - Leviticus 20:8

3. Jehovah Tisdkenu = The Lord Our Righteousness - Jeremiah 23:6
4. Jehovah Nissi = You are our banner - Exodus 17:15
5. Jehovah, the Lord your God= I Am the Lord who Heals - Exodus 15:26

"He is the Lord who heals" is the one I relate to the most. God has healed me in many areas of my life.

God healed me from all of my pass hurt and shame, being in two failed marriages and several failed relationships. I had to totally depend and get more connected to the I Am.

He healed me in 2012. I went through a time in my life where I was diagnosed with congested heart failure. I was hospitalized twice and each time the doctor told me I got there just in time. I know God as a healer.

As of today, the heart doctor has released me. They can't find anything wrong with me. I praise God. He had a plan for my life from the beginning. The devil had a plan that wouldn't work, BUT GOD. He wants to heal, deliver and set us free, so we can fulfill His purpose for our lives.

There will be times when we have our own plans, when our flesh doesn't want to walk in the plan of God. Our plan and God's plan are not one in the same. The Bible tells us that God knows the plan He has for us. In Jeremiah 29:11 (NLT) in reads, "For I know the plans I have for you," says the Lord. "They are plans for good and not for disaster, to give you a future and a hope." God thinks more highly of us than we do ourselves.

First, He may send people over and over to speak into our lives and let us know that he is going to move. Next, he may send others to assure we get it. However, sometimes, when we are in the world, we don't want to hear or see what God is saying or showing us. Most of the time it is because we are enjoying doing what we want to do.

I enjoyed being in the company of people. I enjoyed cooking out, smoking meat on the grill, having fish fries, having lasagna dinners with a movie while drinking Brandy. I enjoyed making homemade wine, smoking cigarettes, and having people at my house. I knew those people were not right for me, so I overlooked their faults to culminate my own needs because at the time, it was all about self and the flesh. I wasn't interested in God's plan.

As time went on, I began going to church more and more. I was looking for something, I didn't know what, but I knew it had to be better than what I was experiencing and doing. I didn't know that I was looking for the "I AM" all along.

I began to realize that you can have all of the nice things and many people around you, and you can try to make all of the money you want, but, without the

"I AM" in your life, you have nothing because you don't have that joy.

What is God Speaking to you about?

_____

_____

_____

_____

_____

_____

_____

_____

_____

_____

_____

_____

_____

_____

_____

_____

_____

_____

_____

_____

_____

The Voice of Jesus

When you really learn the voice of Jesus and how He spoke in scripture. You will recognize that when he spoke, He spoke with authority, and it was in His voice. Jesus spoke about Him being the "I Am." Jesus spoke the way God spoke, and we have the same authority to speak the same way. Let's look at some of those verses.

<u>Scripture Reference:</u>

"Jesus said to them, "I am the bread of life; whoever comes to me shall not hunger, and whoever believes in me shall never thirst." John 6:35 (ESV)

"Again, Jesus spoke to them saying, "I am the light of the world. Whoever follows me will not walk in darkness but will have the light of life." John 8:12 (ESV)

"I am the door. If anyone enters by me, he will be saved and will go in and out and find pasture." John 10:9 (ESV)

"I am the good shepherd. The good shepherd lays down his life for the sheep. John 10:11 (ESV)

"Jesus said to her, "I am the resurrection and the life. Whoever believes in me, though he die, yet shall he live, and everyone who lives and believes in me shall never die. Do you believe this? John 11:25-26 (ESV)

"Jesus said to him, "I am the way, and the truth, and the life. No one comes to the Father except through me." John 14:6 (ESV)

"I am the vine; you are the branches. Whoever abides in me and I in him, it is he that bears much fruit, for apart from me you can do nothing." John: 15:5 (ESV)

Jesus spoke what God spoke, both of them being the "I Am." We are also the "I am." When we walk away from our past, we leave the "I Was" and walk in the "I Am" with the Father. Let's take a look at the "I Am" that we must speak over our lives.

Scripture Reference:
"And the Lord shall make thee the head, and not the tail; and thou shalt be above only, and thou shalt not be beneath; if that thou hearken unto the commandments of the Lord thy God, which I command thee this day, to observe and to do them." Deuteronomy 28 :13 (KJV)

Speak:

"I am the head and not the tail."

"I am above and not beneath."

"I am blessed."

"I am chosen."

"I am wealthy."

"I am awesome."

"I am thankful."

"I am victorious."

"I am redeemed by the blood."

"I am more than a conqueror."

"I am the temple of the Christ."

"I am the light of the world."

"I am a new creation."

"I am walking in love."

"I am up and not down.

"I am more than enough."

"I am the salt of the earth."

"I am walking in peace."

"I am courageous."

"I am beautiful."

"I am worthy."

"I am whole."

"I am wise."

"I Am."

To whom God says, "I Am," speak the I am in your own life.

Jesus laid the foundation for the "I AM" in your life. Will you receive them for you and your family today? Explain.

_____

_____

_____

_____

_____

_____

_____

_____

_____

_____

_____

_____

_____

_____

_____

_____

CHAPTER 8
KNOW THE TRUTH ABOUT YOU

Now that you understand a little of the truth about God and receiving His son as your savior, you should feel good about yourself. This is where you should know the truth about yourself and who you belong to.

You will continue to learn the truth through His word and the teachings of God. As you begin to follow His teaching, you will learn more about who He is and how you fit in His plan. In addition, you will learn all about the love He has for you.

The teaching of God is very simple. Some people want you to think God is difficult. God is all about us worshipping and praising him. He wants us to be loving, to share with others, to have peace, to be good to ourselves, our families, and to be obedient. Are you aware that your family is your first ministry? However, sometimes they don't always receive us, but we always have to show them the Love of God. It must flow from us to them. There are going to be times that some family members will make you angry, but you must still show them the love of God and move on. They need to see the God in you. Therefore, always carry yourself as God would desire.

Let's take a look at the Fruit of The Spirit!

"But the fruit of the Spirit is love, joy, peace, patience, kindness, goodness, faithfulness, gentleness, self-control; against such things there is no law. Galatians 5:22-23 (ESV)

We must always walk in the way of Christ, never shaming Him because we are His representatives in the earth. The truth should always be before us as we walk upright before Him, learning His word and His ways. He reveals Himself differently at different times. Spend time in His presence and allow Him to open up to you.

Now that I know the truth, I can...

_____

_____

_____

_____

_____

_____

_____

_____

_____

_____

_____

_____

_____

_____

_____

_____

_____

_____

_____

CHAPTER 9
STEPPING INTO THE "I AM"

Accepting who God says I am

When we step into the "I Am," we need to see ourselves as Christ sees us. We need to accept what God is saying about us. The Bible tells us that we are a new creature when we come to Him. The old has passed away, and the New has begun.

"Therefore, if anyone is in Christ, he is a new creation. The old has passed away;

behold, the new has come. 2 Corinthians 5:17 (ESV)

In my experience, I have learned if you want to live your life to the fullest, you have to be willing to walk away from the "I Was" and turn your life over to God. Please understand, we will never reach the point where there will never be any problems in our lives. There will always be something to deal with, such as generational issues. There will be memories of our past, but the good thing about it is we don't have to do it alone. We have the Holy Spirit of Christ.

When you pray about your circumstances, have faith that your prayer has been heard, and you are free. He doesn't always move the thorns;

sometimes the thorns remain, but His grace is still sufficient. When you pray, believe it. If He doesn't move it, continue to walk in His grace. He will grant you the power and the strength to go through it. God is the judge, and He has appointed you and anointed you for service.

"But he said to me, "My grace is sufficient for you, for my power is made perfect in weakness." Therefore, I will boast all the more gladly of my weaknesses, so that the power of Christ may rest upon me. 2 Corinthians 12:9 (ESV) "that according to the riches of his glory he may grant you to be strengthened with power through his Spirit in your inner being," Ephesians 3:16 (ESV)

"I thank him who has given me strength, Christ Jesus our Lord, because he judged me faithful, appointing me to his service," 1 Timothy 1: 12 (ESV)

When you look at the "I Am" God, He is not a big Block of ICE where you come and chisel off some pieces when you feel you are dried up. God is the WATER. He will you give you a drink when you are thirsty. We don't have to work hard by chiseling the ICE to get water when He can meet your need and give you a gallon of water, and you won't ever thirst again. You will be refreshed, restored and rebuilt.

We are united with Christ, and we will join Him in the air someday. It doesn't matter what people say; we are connected with the Father and connected with Christ by our faith. You have been made whole. You have efficiently walked away from the "I Was." You are now walking in the "I AM." You have been washed with the blood of Jesus.

"But he who is joined to the Lord becomes one spirit with him. Corinthians 6: 17 (ESV)

What has changed in your life, and what are you expecting God to do in the "I AM?"

_____

_____

_____

_____

_____

_____

_____

_____

_____

_____

_____

_____

_____

_____

_____

_____

_____

Accepting Who God Says You Are

The following verses will help you along your journey.

1. God has created you to be more and more like Him; He has made you In His image.

"So God created man in his own image, in the image of God he created him; male and female he created them." Genesis 1: 27 (ESV)

2. God loves us so much that He gave His only Son for our sin so that we can have eternal life.

""For God so loved the world, that he gave his only Son, that whoever believes in him should not perish but have eternal life." John 3:16 (ESV)

3. God has covered our sins; He's loved us through His Son, so love others as He has loved you.

"Above all, keep loving one another earnestly, since love covers a multitude of sins." 1 Peter 4: 8 (ESV)

4. You are a masterpiece made by God; you are wonderfully made.

"I praise you, for I am fearfully and wonderfully made. Wonderful are your works; my soul knows it very well." Psalms 139:14 (ESV)

5. We can't do anything without God because in Him is where we receive the strength that we need.

"I can do all things through him who strengthens me. Philippians 4: 13 (ESV)

6. God shows us His love even when we are sinners. He allows Christ to stand in the gap for us.

"but God shows his love for us in that while we were still sinners, Christ died for us." Romans 5:8 (ESV)

7. The children of God have that access to Christ because we are one with Him when we accept Him.

"For through him we both have access in one Spirit to the Father." Ephesians 2:18 (ESV)

8. We have been filled with the Spirit of Christ. All authorities and powers are in God's hand.

"and you have been filled in him, who is the head of all rule and authority. Colossians 2:10 (ESV)

CHAPTER 10
WALKING IN YOUR INHERITANCE, THE "I AM"

Once I received Christ, I stepped out of the "I Was." I immediately became an heir of God and a co-heir with Christ. I am the seed of Abraham. You have the same benefits. Our inheritance doesn't start two weeks after we receive Christ; it starts when we allow God to come into our lives.

When we receive Christ, we inherit the wealth of God. The most important inheritance is salvation and faith. Jesus went to the cross so that we might be free from the "I Was" of our past.

In other words, once you give your life over to Him, you gain it all. You are probably asking how. I'm glad you asked.

God has it all! Everything on the earth, He spoke it out of His mouth. When he created mankind, he spoke as well, but he also worked. He said, "Let us make man in our own image." He wanted us to be a part of what he had created. For six days, He created the earth and man, and then He rested. He gave it all to Adam and Eve. He desired for Eve to also enjoy His creation. Yes, each time God has proved Himself to man, even when man has messed up.

When we look at the book of Noah, we see that God wanted us to have the best, but the world was sinful, and He destroyed it all and started all over again. God had Himself a son threw Mary and gave Him up as a sacrifice so we would be able to live here on this earth and walk in the inheritance each and every day. The sin brought about death, so He allowed His Son to go to the cross. Now, we can live again as He had planned from the beginning. When we read the books of the Bible, from Genesis throughout, there is nothing but wealth. Therefore, if you have a Father that has all of this wealth and He owns everything, do you believe He is not going to allow you to walk into your inheritance. You don't have to wait for someone to pass away in your family to receive what they might want to leave; you can walk in it every day.

When God sent Jesus to the cross, it was for healing in all areas of our lives, not just for the body but for wherever we have been wounded and broken in our spirit.

Some people today believe being poor and without is the will of God, but God doesn't want us to leave what He has for us on the shelf hidden in a closet, and we never have access to it. Ask yourself, "Why would God want you to live poor if He is rich? He is our Father, and He wants us to have what he has already put aside for us because He knew we were coming. He knew us before we were formed in our mother's womb. God wants us to prosper in His word as our soul prospers. We need to receive what He has for us. We have all that we need; we just need to activate the promises of God, then nothing can stop us, no matter what things look like or feel like.

Scripture Reference:

"And now that you belong to Christ, you are the true children of Abraham. You are his heirs, and God's promise to Abraham belongs to you." Galatians 3:29 (NLT)

"But he was pierced because of our rebellion, crushed because of our iniquities; punishment for our peace was on him, and we are healed by his wounds." Isaiah 53: 5 (CSB)

You are walking in the inheritance of
The
"I AM:"

Walking in Your Salvation
Walking in Love
Walking in Joy
Walking by Faith
Walking in Wealth
Walking in Health
Walking in Peace
Walking in Prosperity
Walk into your inheritance every day!

Write down more of your inheritance that you are choosing to walk in.

_____

_____

_____

_____

_____

_____

_____

_____

_____

_____

_____

_____

_____

_____

_____

_____

_____

_____

_____

Walking Away from the "I Was" into the "I Am" Prayer

Father, I ask that you forgive me for my sins, hidden sins that I might not be aware of. I want to thank you for what you have done and for the things you will continue to do. I am so grateful for what you are doing in my life. I thank you for making me fearfully and wonderfully made.

I am the head and not the tail. I am above and not beneath. I am wealthy, and I have more than enough. I am healthy, and I walk in the abundance of love, joy, and peace. I thank you that I no longer walk in the "I Was" of the past. I am a new creation; I walk in you, the "I A M." I am more than a conqueror. I can do all things threw you, Christ Jesus, that strengthens me. I am wise in my decision making. You have given me the wisdom that I need. I have been set free and redeemed from the curse of the enemy. I have all I need, and I'm walking in my inheritance every day. I'm walking in prosperity, and nothing can stop me. In the name of Jesus I pray, Amen.

"Don't you know that the unrighteous will not inherit God's kingdom? Do not be deceived: No sexually immoral people, idolaters, adulterers, or males who have sex with males, no thieves, greedy people, drunkards, verbally abusive people, or swindlers will inherit God's kingdom.

1 Corinthians 6: 9-10 (CSB)

Write your own Prayer

_____

_____

_____

_____

_____

_____

_____

_____

_____

_____

_____

_____

_____

_____

_____

_____

_____

_____

_____

Write Your own Prayer

_____

_____

_____

_____

_____

_____

_____

_____

_____

_____

_____

_____

_____

_____

_____

_____

_____

_____

_____

_____

I would like to thank each and every last one of you for your support. May the blessings of God rain down on you, your family, friends, and loved ones. I pray that you will walk in greatness.

Pastor Brenda T. Vaughn

Let me hear in the morning of your
steadfast love, for in you I trust. Make
me know the way I should go, for to you
I lift up my soul.
Psalms 143:8 (ESV)

Author

BRENDA T. VAUGHN

www.ingramcontent.com/pod-product-compliance
Lightning Source LLC
Chambersburg PA
CBHW060946040426
42445CB00011B/1026